Mapperley an(
with Woodboro

on old picture ┌ ... ──

Grenville Jennings

WESLEYAN CHAPEL
MANSFIELD ROAD, NOTTINGHAM.

1. The imposing Wesleyan Chapel at the corner of Mansfield Road and Woodborough Road, which opened in 1874 and hosted its last service in May 1973. *"This is the church where I go"*, wrote the sender of a 'Clumber' series postcard to Grantham in January 1911.

**Designed and Published by
Reflections of a Bygone Age,
Keyworth, Nottingham
1995**
Revised edition March 1999

£3.50

-1-

St. Andrew's Church School c.1917. This was situated on the corner of Bangor Street and Alfred Street North, off Woodborough Road.

Printed by
Adlard Print and Typesetting Services,
Ruddington, Notts.

ISBN 1 900138 02 6

Front cover: a superb picture postcard from the 1920s in the 'Rex' series, showing a busy Mansfield Road, Sherwood. Marshall Street is on the right.
Back cover (top): a rural-looking Mapperley Plains on a 'Clumber' series card of 1905, showing the premises of D. Ward, grocers, on the left.
            (bottom): Cavendish Vale, Sherwood, on a 'Peveril' postcard of the early 1920s.

Acknowledgements: I'd like to thank Peter Cooke for the loan of illustrations 21-23, 47 and 55; and to Nic and Marion Church for illustrations 4, 9, 17-19, 26, 29-30, 42 and 54.

WOODBOROUGH ROAD, NOTTINGHAM.

2. Woodborough Road Baptist Chapel, built at a cost of £7,500 by Watson Fothergill for the church trustees. Opened in 1894 by Thos. Bayley M.P., it seated 900 people, and is seen here on a c.1905 'Clumber' series card. Alfred Street North runs off to the left. The building is now used as the 'Pakistan Centre'.

INTRODUCTION

As we approach the millennium, it is with great diffidence that many of us look over our shoulder into the past and wonder what life was like in our respective town or village at the turn of the century. For those who do share this feeling of how our forefathers lived and how our respective suburb looked in those early days we must thank the publishers of the picture postcard.

The purpose of this book is to portray Woodborough Road, Mapperley and Sherwood through the medium of picture postcards, which were at the height of their popularity in Edwardian times – both as items on which to send messages and as pictures to collect.

Picture postcards were first published in Britain in 1894, but it was not until a decade later that they began to take off, when in 1902 the Post Office allowed a message to be written on the address side. This meant that the whole of one side was available for the picture, which obviously gave more scope to the publishers of postcards.

Photographic viewcards became very popular and the postcard provided the most important way of communicating news or messages in much the same way as the telephone is used today. The years up to 1914 were the `Golden Age' of picture postcards, when millions of cards portraying every imaginable subject were published by a host of national and local firms. Hardly a village or hamlet was not documented at that time by a postcard publisher, though sometimes the number of cards available was unrelated to the size of a community.

Views of Nottingham City centre, the Castle, Arboretum and Trent Bridge were profusely covered by the publishing giants, Valentine of Dundee, Raphael Tuck and W.H. Smith as to be quite common, but for areas such as Mapperley and Sherwood it was mainly local publishers such as Albert Hindley, `Peveril' Series, W.H. Smith, `Rex' Series and amateur photographers on whom we must rely for our glimpse into the past.

Albert Hindley was the most prolific local publisher around 1905, working from his stationery shop in Clumber Street, Nottingham (currently occupied by Granada TV Rentals). He published cards in the `Clumber' Series, covering most of Nottingham and the surrounding area. These cards were printed in colour by a firm in Glasgow, though postcards were printed later as black and white real photographs.

Another exceptionally fine publisher was C. & A.G. Lewis, whose photographic cards were published nationally, but with a good local cross-section of cards, mostly in the 1920's.

In the main, most cards produced were of well-known locations and main thoroughfares. There are many exceptions to the rule and when a view of a side street or a local event is discovered, then the pleasure to the collector is immeasurable. One negative factor is that many of the cards produced show relatively empty streets. Indeed it was sometimes only with the help of local children that the photographer was able to provide some animation.

The views themselves provide endless fascination, with a further bonus of the message on the back. We must thank those early pioneers who produced a fascinating and accurate record of the era, and all those people who preserved the cards for us to enjoy some ninety years later.

Grenville Jennings
November 1995

3. An anonymously-published postcard from the early 1920s, looking down Woodborough Road from Peashill Road/Carnarvon Street. On the left are the shops of J. France (boot repairer), Holmes (picture framers) and Leatherland (decorators).

4. An extremely scarce postcard of the "Marquis of Hastings" public house, showing landlady Elizabeth Ratcliffe on the corner of Carnarvon Street and Marple Street in the 1920s. An electrical firm, Camms, used the building in the 1960s, while in the following decade, it was demolished completely as part of a slum clearance programme.

5. Tram no. 142 passes the Emanuel Church (on the left) on its way up the hilly Woodborough Road in the 1930s. The Mapperley tram route was the most difficult of all the Nottingham routes with a steepest gradient of 1 in 11$\frac{1}{2}$.

St. Augustine's R.C. Church, Woodborough Road, Nottingham. No. 2355.

6. A postcard published by local firm C. & A.G. Lewis of St. Augustine's Roman Catholic Church on Woodborough Road. The card was sent to Bristol in August 1922.

7. Woodborough Road showing the "Enterprise Hotel", another of the properties demolished as part of slum clearance in the 1970s. Northville Street goes off to the right. Card published in the 'Peveril' series, and posted to North London in 1913.

WOODBOROUGH ROAD, NOTTINGHAM

8. No traffic problems on Woodborough Road in pre-First World War days. Another 'Peveril' series postcard.

CORPORATION OAKS ENTRANCE, WOODBOROUGH ROAD

9. The entrance to Corporation Oaks, Woodborough Road, on a card published in the 'Peveril' series c.1910. The view is little changed today.

176   ROBIN HOOD'S CHASE, NOTTINGHAM.

10. Robin Hood's Chase ran from Woodborough Road to St. Ann's Well Road, with the entrance opposite Corporation Oaks. A postcard published by W.H. Smith, sent to a private serving with the Sherwood Foresters on camp in Galway, Ireland, in the first weeks of the First World War. The chase is still a footpath.

11. The entrance to Alexandra Park on a 'Peveril' series card, showing a c.1910 scene. A block of flats, Alexandra Court, now stands behind the building featured here, which is almost unchanged today.

Alexandra Park School, 249 Woodborough Rd., Nottingham.
Principal Mr. F. Payne B. A. (London).

12. Alexandra Park School gymnastics team is featured on this multi-view card published by The Freckleton Studio.

13. An extremely rural scene in Alexandra Park about 1904, seen on a postcard published by the London firm Blum & Degen. More properties have been built on this land during the past 90 years.

203   MAPPERLEY HILL, NOTTINGHAM.

14. Tramcar no.120 descending the difficult Mapperley Hill en route for Trent Bridge via the Market Place. Card published by W.H. Smith c.1910.

15. Looking down Woodborough Road from the top of Mapperley Hill, a city-bound tram can be seen in the distance on a 1920s 'Rex' series postcard sent to Mablethorpe.

16. St. Jude's Church, Mapperley, built in 1877 at a cost of £3,000 to seat a congregation of 285. Anonymously-published card, sent to Loughborough in July 1910. A newly-built centre adjacent to the church is host to a wide range of community groups.

17. St. Jude's Parish Mission on a postcard sent to Grantham in August 1910.

18. St. Jude's Avenue, off Woodborough Road. This view can hardly have had a wide interest, for the avenue was a dead end! The card was posted to Bristol in March 1912, sending birthday wishes. One of the street's residents was wealthy enough to afford a motor car. The embryo trees that have just been planted are today much more in evidence!

19. Very little has changed here since this card was published (by the same photographer as illus. 18) in 1912.

Tram Terminus, Mapperley.

20. Mapperley Tram Terminus on a postcard published by W.H. Smith during the First World War. The billboard on the left advertises *"Sir J. French reports British success"*. The view is looking towards Porchester Road.

Mapperley Terminus, Nottingham.

21. A later view of the terminus in the early 1920s on 'Rex' series card no.183. Note the barber's pole on the left, the two trams in the background, and Eaton Street, going off to the right. The writer of the card comments *"our house is 3 minutes from this point and is 420 feet above sea level, and quite in the country."*

Rex Series:- No. 183

22. An earlier view of the terminus on a 'Clumber' series card of c.1906, featuring tramcar no.100. The photograph was taken from the corner of Porchester Road, with the Wesleyan chapel in the background. The Mapperley route was extended to Westdale Lane on 7th June 1926, and finally closed in February 1936.

23. Mapperley Plains in the early 1920s on a card published by C. & A.G. Lewis and sent to Whittlesea in Cambridgeshire. The well-made road was so quiet that the boys on the left could stand there in confidence!

24. The war memorial at the corner of Woodthorpe Drive, Mapperley, seen on a 'Rex' series card of the early 1920s. The property in the background, at the top of Whittingham Road, was sold for development in the latter part of 1997. For many years it was the home of the Long family, whose business advert was *"we long to dye for you"*.

25. The "Westdale Tea Rooms" just edges on to this 'Clumber' series card of 1906, intended to feature the view looking down Westdale Lane. The County Library is on the left of this location today.

26. A splendid postcard view of the "Westdale Tea Rooms" 1908. The sender of the card was actually staying here extremely busy road junction at this spot. The building still on the right now hosts an estate agency.

ed by W.R. Norwood, on the corner of Westdale Lane in
e time. This rural scene contrasts sharply with today's
;, now occupied by two different shops, and an extension

27. A view of Mapperley Plains in 1922 on a card published by C. & A.G. Lewis. The road, devoid of traffic, is being used exclusively by pedestrians and as a playground: note the boy with the hoop!

28. The 'new' tram terminus in the late 1920s on 'Rex' series postcard no.262. Gretton Road is on the right.

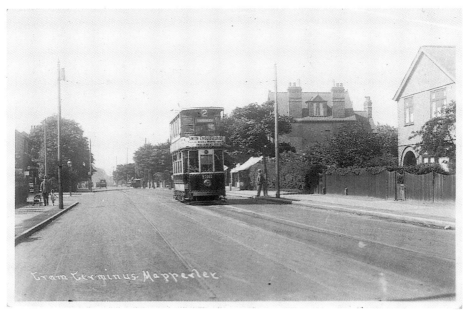

29. A fine view of tramcar no. 136 at the Westdale Lane tram terminus on a postcard by local publisher Spree. Note the advertising on the tram in both this and the previous illustration.

30. Mapperley Schools in 1910 on a postcard sent to Grantham. The poster on the school wall advises that the Froebel Society were holding a display of 'Old English Graces', including morris dancing, in the near future.

31. Mapperley in 1910. A view on the Plains Road.

32. A card by the same anonymous publisher showing a scene on Mapperley Plains Road looking in the opposite direction (towards Nottingham) from the card above. Note the early motor-car, obviously one of the first in the area.

CORONATION BONFIRE MAPPERLEY 1911.

33. This bonfire, for the coronation celebrations of King George V on 22nd June 1911, was sited on the highest point of the Nottingham Patent Brick Company's premises. It is being carefully guarded by three local policemen!

MANSFIELD ROAD, NOTTINGHAM.

34. Tram no.111 on route no.1 (Market Place-Sherwood) moves along Mansfield Road, Sherwood. The supporting centre poles for the overhead wire proved most difficult for other motor vehicles to negotiate. Card published by W.H. Smith in 1910.

CARRINGTON CHURCH, NOTTINGHAM.

35. St. John's Church on Mansfield Road, built in 1841. 'Clumber' series postcard of 1905.

36. Looking down Mansfield Road towards Carrington in 1913 on a W.H. Smith card.

37. Mapperley Hall Drive looking towards Mansfield Road, seen on a 'Peveril' series card of c.1910. Carisbrooke Drive entrance is on the left, while the lady in black is crossing Hatfield Road.

38. One of a series published by A.E. Webster of Haydn Road Post Office. This uninspiring, unanimated view, features Percival Road. It is almost unchanged today, except for the rows of parked cars.

39. Devonshire Road, off Haydn Road. This card was posted to Trowbridge in 1927. Quite a busy scene compared with the previous one! The road is in reality much steeper than it looks on this postcard.

40. This Leyland bus was operated in the 1950s for coach tours by G.H.F. Atkins, 38 Elmswood Gardens, Sherwood.

MANSFIELD ROAD, SHERWOOD, NOTTINGHAM.

41. 'Clumber' series card of 1905 showing tram no.48 passing Private Road en route to Nottingham. Two other trams are visible in the distance. The card was posted to Hartington in Derbyshire in September 1906.

MANSFIELD ROAD. SHERWOOD.

42. Mansfield Road, Sherwood on a card posted to Liverpool in January 1929. On the right are the shops of Alice Sayle (costumier), Lucy Greathead (draper), and Fred Hammond (grocer). Further down are the premises of W. Bamford and Sons, undertaker.

HAYDN ROAD, SHERWOOD.

43. Another card by A.E. Webster, featuring Haydn Road in the late 1920s. This is now a very busy thoroughfare, with lots of parked cars by the roadsides.

44. The tram sheds at Sherwood on an anonymously-published c.1903 photograph. The first electric tram which replaced the horse-drawn vehicles ran from this depot to the Market Place on 1st January 1901. The fare was 2d.

45. Another view of the tram sheds, this time on 'Clumber' series no. 461. The card was sent to Meersbrook in July 1911.

46. Mansfield Road, Sherwood, in the 1920s, portrayed on a C. & A.G. Lewis card, featuring a tram in the distance on route no.1. Note the absence of the central poles for the tramwires *(see illus. 45)*. The advertising hoarding on the right announces *"Elite Picture Theatre now open'*. The card was posted to Trowbridge in July 1927.

oad, Sherwood. No. 2021.

47. Dornoch Avenue off Winchester Street. A late 1920s postcard, published by Spree. This view of the very steep street looks down towards Mansfield Road.

48. Ramsdale Crescent, Sherwood, on a 'Rex' series card posted from Nottingham in June 1922. The Crescent is now attractively tree-lined.

49. The "Robin Hood Hotel" Sherwood, with the premises of J.W. Beasley (ladies wear) on the left, and W. Meakin (chemist/dentist) on the right.

50. Sherwood railway station was the third on the suburban line, opened in 1886 but existing only until 1916 as a passenger line. Sherwood boasted substantial buildings, for the original project to build the line – financed by Nottingham businessmen – was an ambitious one. In the end the passenger service was an early victim of tram competition. 'Clumber' series card, posted to Sutton-on-Sea in October 1905.

51. A view from Sherwood station of the tunnel through Woodthorpe Park that led to Daybrook. Goods traffic continued on the line through to 1951. 'Clumber' series card, posted to Norfolk in August 1908.

52. When the Great Central Railway arrived in Nottingham, the workhouse in York Street was pulled down. Not until 1908 was a new one built on Hucknall Road, Bagthorpe, at a cost of £273,000 to accommodate over 1,700 inmates. Card published by W.H. Smith c.1910.

53. Edwards Lane, Sherwood. The boy on the right is Harold Hindley, son of Albert, publisher of this postcard in the 'Clumber' series. It was posted to Pole Street in Nottingham in September 1909.

54. A later view of Edwards Lane in the 1920s, this time in the C. & A.G. Lewis series. It was posted to Tamworth in May 1933.

55. Daybrook Vale, Sherwood, on a postcard by C. & A.G. Lewis.

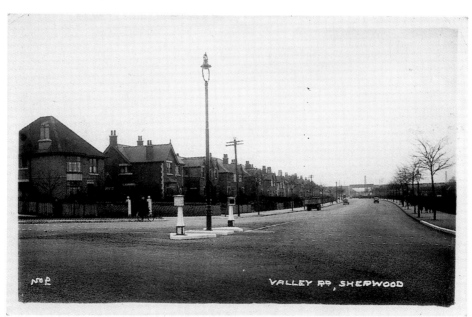

56. Valley Road (now part of the ring road) on a card published by R. Richards of York about 1942. In the distance can be seen the bridge carrying the L.N.E.R. (ex-Great Central) railway line.